Nocturnal
Animals After Dark

Illustrated by Ángel Svoboda
Written by Lucas Riera

Translation from Spanish by Little Gestalten

Typefaces: Exo 2 by Natanael Gama; KoHo by Cadson Demak

Printed by Agpograf, Barcelona, Spain
Made in Europe

Published by Little Gestalten, Berlin, 2023
ISBN 978-3-96704-762-2

The Spanish original edition *Nocturnos* was published by Mosquito Books Barcelona.
© Mosquito Books Barcelona, 2023
© Texts: Lucas Riera, 2023
© Illustrations: Ángel Svoboda, 2023
© for the English edition: Little Gestalten, an imprint of Die Gestalten Verlag GmbH & Co. KG, Berlin 2023.

For more information, and to order books, please visit: www.little.gestalten.com

Bibliographic information published by the Deutsche Nationalbibliothek.
The Deutsche Nationalbibliothek lists this publication in the Deutsche Nationalbibliografie;
detailed bibliographic data are available online at www.dnb.de.

This book was printed on paper certified according to the standards of the FSC®.

MIX
Paper from
responsible sources
FSC® C104592
FSC
www.fsc.org

Lucas Riera · Ángel Svoboda

NOCTURNAL

Animals After Dark

LITTLE
GESTALTEN

In this book you will find . . .

There are two sides to nature. The one we know best lives in the warmth of sunlight, naturally illuminated and full of life. Most animals and plants live their lives during the hours of daylight and follow this rhythm from dawn.

But this book deals with the second part of the day. When dusk comes in, when the Sun goes down, when we ourselves begin to feel tired after a long day, another cycle begins for nature.

Some animals wake up because it is time to hunt. Others sharpen their senses, aware of any movement, ready to hear the slightest sound. While some plants wither, others revive and bloom. The sea changes its rhythm, the Moon shines brightly, and the sky is ablaze with stars.

This book will tell you everything that happens when there is no natural light, when the Sun illuminates the other side of the Earth, and when we cannot see anything in the dark.

Night falls, and the show begins . . .

Sunset in the Jungle

Sunset is the moment when the Sun dips below the horizon, announcing the arrival of the night.

Twilight is the light that we can still see in the sky when the Sun has set. In reality, it is the refraction of the rays on the atmosphere.

Herbivorous mammals cautiously emerge from their hiding places and head for the river bank to drink. Sometimes, predators are crouching in wait for them.

Many insects hide or bury themselves in the ground and remain still.

Most birds build their nests and settle in the shelter of the treetops for the night.

Nocturnal predatory birds, such as owls, take up position and appear motionless, not making any noise, searching for their prey.

Alligators are most active between dusk (the darker stage of twilight) and dawn (the time just before the sunrise).

What Is the Night?

To most of us, night time is when we go to sleep. When the Sun goes down and we start to feel tired, we take advantage of the darkness and go to bed.

But are all nights the same length? And are they always dark?

As the Earth turns on its axis, only one half of it can be illuminated at once. This means that half of the planet is dark while the other is bathed in light.

HOURS OF DAYLIGHT ACROSS THE WORLD

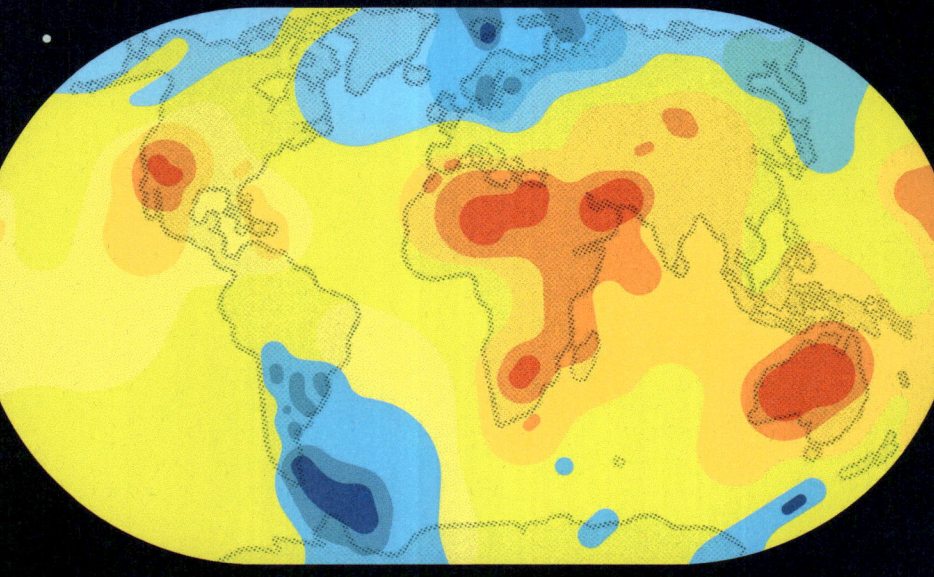

- 4,000
- 3,600
- 3,000
- 2,600
- 2,200
- 1,800
- 1,300
- 900
- 400

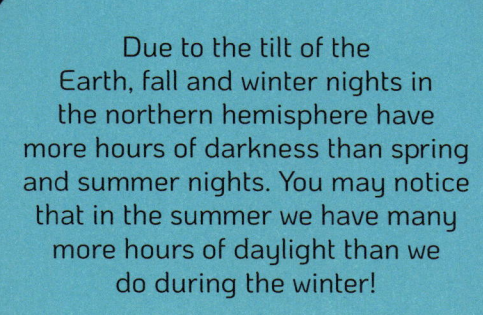

Due to the tilt of the Earth, fall and winter nights in the northern hemisphere have more hours of darkness than spring and summer nights. You may notice that in the summer we have many more hours of daylight than we do during the winter!

Have you ever noticed that the Sun always rises in one place and sets in another? It is not actually the Sun that is rising or falling, it is just that the planet has turned on its axis, making it seem that way!

Humans, like most other living beings on the planet, are diurnal animals. This means that we mainly live our lives while the Sun is out in the part of the world we live in, and we use the night time to rest and regain our energy.

In this book we are going to look at what happens when the Sun sets and the light disappears. During the night you can see incredible natural phenomena, like the northern lights and high tides, and there are many animals and plants that follow a different rhythm to ours. When we go to bed, they wake up and go about their lives.

Nocturnal Birds

If you are a fan of birds, you will know that a lot of them live a life very similar to ours: for them, sunlight is the natural accompaniment to their lives. They wake up very early, just before daybreak, and usually use the night to sleep, or at least to rest and stay still.

But some kinds of birds behave in the opposite way. Night falls in the forest, and many owls take up their positions to hunt. Did you know that owls have lived on Earth for around 65 million years? Although there are many species, they all have large eyes, can turn their heads 270 degrees, fly without making the slightest noise, and have extremely sensitive hearing.

Moorish owl

Great horned owl

Jamaican owl

American eagle owl

Owl's eyes are specially adapted to see in low light.

Northern hawk-owl (*Surnia ulula*)

It is so called because although it is a nocturnal raptor, it is actually very similar to a hawk or falcon! It has long pointed wings, a long tail, and a flattened head.

Austral pygmy owl (*Glaucidium nana*)

It is small but very fierce. It can hunt animals bigger than itself. When it flies it does not make any noise.

West Solomon's owl

This species of nocturnal raptor have survived for so long thanks to their incredible ability to adapt to many different habitats. Some species can live in icy landscapes, while others inhabit desert areas.

They have evolved by perfecting their nocturnal hunting skills: they often remain motionless, blending in with their surroundings, watching, until their prey unknowingly approaches.

Predatory Mammals

Animals (and humans) have evolved over thousands of years to adapt to the environment in which they live and survive. Some animals have developed the ability to see in extremely low light—almost complete darkness! Their eyes have special adaptations that allow this; some through size, some because of the amount of light they let in, and some using thermal vision.

The bat is the only flying mammal. They are extremely important to their environments, helping to maintain ecological balance and biodiversity. Almost all bats are nocturnal.

The pupil is a part of the eye that opens or closes to capture light and send it to the retina.

GOAT   HORSE   CAT   LEMUR   HUMAN

A bat's eyes are designed so that they are able to capture the faintest, even "invisible" rays of light. It's a good system for hunting!

The Andean night monkey (*Aotus lemurinus*) is a small primate that has adapted to nocturnal activity, sleeping through the daytime and most active at the beginning of the night.

Bats, like some species of dolphins, use a system called echolocation where they use sound, rather than sight, to locate objects. These high-frequency sounds bounce off objects around them, returning to them and allowing them to understand and exactly pinpoint different objects. This allows them to hunt insects at full speed.

The Iberian Lynx (*Lynux pardinus*) is nocturnal in the summer, but in the winter they can be active during the daytime. They have synched their activity patterns with their main source of prey, the rabbit.

Many of the large predators of the savannah also take advantage of the low light at dusk to hide and wait for their prey.

Who Sees What at Night?

Cats, dogs, deer, and many other animals can see well—even in semi-darkness, because their retina has a layer of cells that works like a mirror to reflect the light. This is why cat's eyes appear to glow in the dark . . .

The tarsier is a small primate that lives in Indonesia. It has huge eyes compared to its body, which allows it to hunt insects and spiders at night.

The owl is one of the animals that can see best at night, thanks to their enormous pupils that allow even the tiniest amount of light to enter. On the other hand, they do not see very well up close.

The dangerous mantis shrimp has the most complex and impressive eyes on the planet! Each of their eyes can see independently from the other and they are able to see three times as many colors as human eyes do.

The eyes of dragonflies take up almost their entire head! They are filled with cells that allow them to capture light as well as movement. Each facet of the eye points in a different direction, giving them the ability to see 360 degrees.

Who Makes So Much Noise at Night?

Crickets and grasshoppers are closely related, but while grasshoppers are active during the day, crickets come out at dusk. Crickets move very quickly along the ground, and live almost anywhere, from forests to marshlands and beaches.

Crickets can chirp at all hours, but particularly on warm nights, when the males rub their wings together to attract females. They love to live near ponds in humid environments, but like insects, they adapt to most habitats . . . there is even a species of domestic cricket which can sneak into houses and live right under our noses!

Cicadas also make their own music. Their peculiar sound is produced by a special organ called a tymbal. A cicada's tymbal is made up of many rib-like structures that make clicking noises when the cicada flexes their muscles.

Although the instrument cicadas play is different, the goal of the music is the same: to attract females.

Crickets have compound eyes, which let them see in all directions. They also have three smaller eyes on their foreheads, called ocelli, which help them tell the difference between light and darkness.

Nocturnal Insects

Thousands of species of insect begin their activity—or are especially active—during the sunset hours and at night. Insects use lots of different senses and adaptations to hunt, mate, and explore at night. For many nocturnal insects, sight is not their most important sense . . .

More flying insects are nocturnal than any other type of insect.

Moths are similar to butterflies, but they are mostly nocturnal. This is why a lot of moths are much less colorful than butterflies.

Moths fold their wings to the sides, covering their bodies.

The hummingbird hawk-moth (*Macroglossum stellatarum*) is a very fast flier. It gets its name because it looks so much like a hummingbird!

If you stare at the wings of the little night curassow (*Saturnia pavonia*), it may make you think that you are being watched by haunting eyes.

Hundreds of cockroaches and beetles live very close to us, but we rarely see them. They can detect movement or air currents caused by other animals, and quickly flee when they detect the slightest risk.

The vast majority of nocturnal Lepidoptera (the taxonomic order of insects that includes butterflies and moths) have dark wings and a hairy body.

Sphinx moths get their name because, as caterpillars, they poke their heads up, which make them look like the Sphinx in Egypt.

23

Moths

Though moths look a lot like butterflies, there are many differences between them. Moths play a big part in the ecosystems they live in and are a very important food source for lots of other animals, like bats, birds, and spiders. There are around 160,000 species of moths in the world (and around 17,500 species of butterflies).

Like butterflies, moths go through a process called metamorphosis, where they turn from a caterpillar into their final form. This starts when the female lays her eggs, and goes through four stages: egg, larva, pupa, and adult.

Moths can become much larger than butterflies. The largest we know of is called the Atlas moth (*Attacus Atlas*). It lives in Asia and can measure up to 10.5 in (27 cm).

Moths are usually excellent pollinators, which means that they transport pollen from plants, which then sticks to the next plant they visit. This allows the plant to be fertilized, creating more fruit or seeds and therefore, more plants and flowers!

Other notable characteristics of moths:

Their very developed sense of smell, using pheromones to smell prey and even mates.

Their long tongue, which allows them to feed on the nectar of some flowers with tube-shaped petals.

Their ability to camouflage: during the day they perch on trees and bushes, and it is almost impossible to distinguish them from their surroundings.

Blind Animals

Many species of animal do not rely on vision to survive. Some of them have very poorly developed eyes and very poor vision. Some animals lack eyes completely, such as the sea urchin or many types of earthworm. Not all of them are nocturnal animals, but they do all have one thing in common—they do not need to see sunlight to survive.

Hedgehogs are not blind, but they do have rather poor vision. They can identify shapes and some colors, but can't see very much detail.

The mole lives underground and usually feeds on earthworms, so it has evolved to not need to see. It has eyes, but they are almost completely covered by skin.

Worms are eyeless invertebrates that live underground and breathe through their skin, so they always seek moist, humid areas of the earth to live in.

Sea urchins don't have eyes, but they can still see! They have special cells in their feet which can detect light.

There are many species of fish that are blind or have very poor vision, such as the Mexican tetra (*Astyanax exicanus*). They live in areas without light, so they have had to develop their other senses to survive.

The Texas blind salamander (*Eurycea rathbuni*) is an amphibian who likes the cold and the dark. These rare creatures live in dark caves and have no eyes, just two black dots under the skin.

Nocturnal Flowers

Flowers need sunlight to survive. But why? And does this apply to all the flowers on Earth?

All plants require sunlight for photosynthesis (the process by which plants use sunlight, water, and carbon dioxide to create oxygen and energy) but some of them are more active at night, because they are pollinated by nocturnal creatures, such as moths.

Among the nocturnal flowers there are many cacti, such as the Queen of the Night (*Epiphyllum oxypetalum*), some species of orchid, and a kind of flowering plant called Datura.

Nocturnal flowers are usually white or light-colored, to make them easier to see in the dark. They also tend to have a stronger smell, again helping them to be found in the dark. These flowers also produce more nectar in the evenings, making them more attractive to the kinds of animals that will help them pollinate, like bats and moths.

Tides

We all know the tides: the rise and fall of the oceans' water levels due to the gravity of the Moon. High tide is when the water level is at its highest, and low tide is when it's at its lowest.

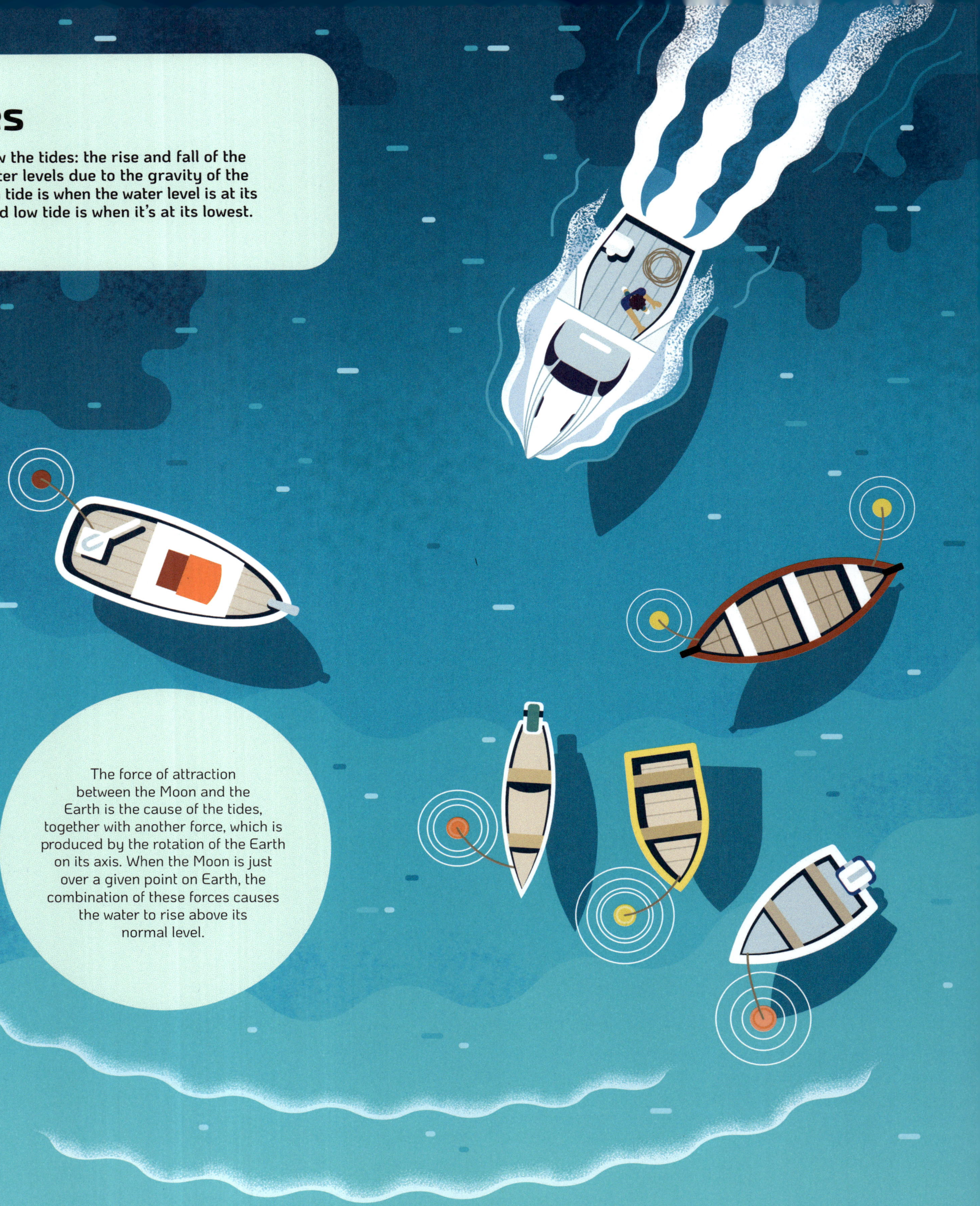

The force of attraction between the Moon and the Earth is the cause of the tides, together with another force, which is produced by the rotation of the Earth on its axis. When the Moon is just over a given point on Earth, the combination of these forces causes the water to rise above its normal level.

The tides are not a phenomenon that occur only at night, but that the tide rises at night and the Moon, especially the full Moon, plays an important role in this phenomenon.

Deep Sea Fish

Some animals do not have to adapt to the night, because their entire lives are spent in a habitat without sunlight, where the rays barely penetrate the thousands of feet of depth of the oceans. Scientists sometimes call these unknown places "chasms."

We know more about the surface of the Moon than we do about the deepest depths of the oceans! The Mariana Trench is the deepest point on Earth, and can be found in the Pacific Ocean. The deepest point is nearly 7 mi (11 km) from the surface. Only six people have ever reached the bottom of the trench, in specially designed underwater vehicles.

Slender snipe eel (Nemichthys scolopaceus)

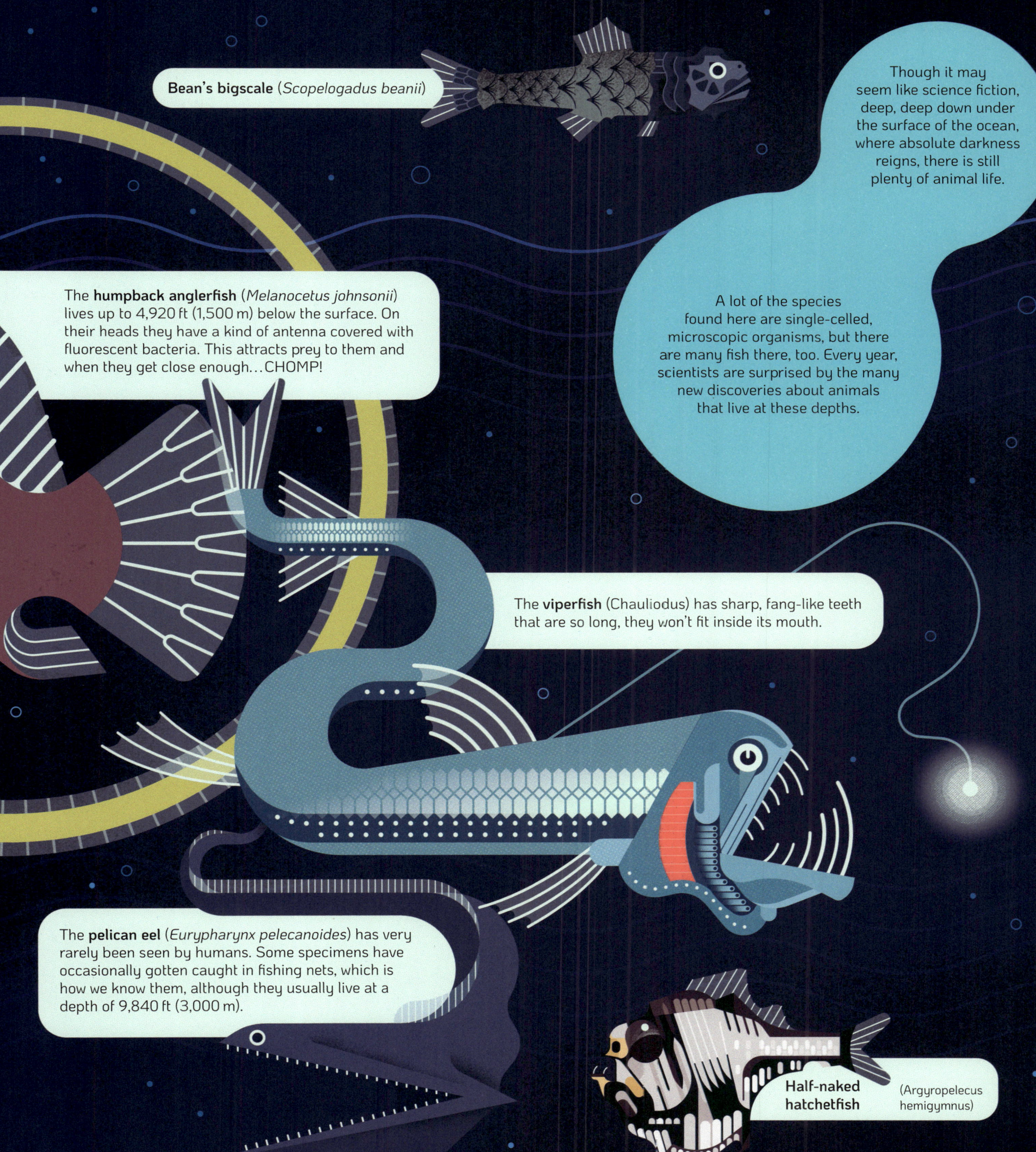

Bean's bigscale (*Scopelogadus beanii*)

Though it may seem like science fiction, deep, deep down under the surface of the ocean, where absolute darkness reigns, there is still plenty of animal life.

The **humpback anglerfish** (*Melanocetus johnsonii*) lives up to 4,920 ft (1,500 m) below the surface. On their heads they have a kind of antenna covered with fluorescent bacteria. This attracts prey to them and when they get close enough…CHOMP!

A lot of the species found here are single-celled, microscopic organisms, but there are many fish there, too. Every year, scientists are surprised by the many new discoveries about animals that live at these depths.

The **viperfish** (Chauliodus) has sharp, fang-like teeth that are so long, they won't fit inside its mouth.

The **pelican eel** (*Eurypharynx pelecanoides*) has very rarely been seen by humans. Some specimens have occasionally gotten caught in fishing nets, which is how we know them, although they usually live at a depth of 9,840 ft (3,000 m).

Half-naked hatchetfish (*Argyropelecus hemigymnus*)

Animals of Light

One of the most amazing phenomena in the natural world is bioluminescence, which is the ability of some species to produce their own light.

There are about 2,000 different species of fireflies on Earth, which produce light thanks to a special organ called a "lantern" which contains cells that create a chemical reaction. They seem to use light to attract mates, and each species has a unique flashing and glowing pattern.

Adult scorpions, especially after the third molt (when they shed their exoskeleton), can emit light when they are exposed to ultraviolet rays—they look like they are glowing!

The firefly squid (*Watasenia scintillans*) is around the size of a human finger, lives a thousand feet under the sea, and emits an intense blue light. Once a year, when these animals travel up to the surface to spawn, they create an incredible natural spectacle.

Some species of jellyfish, such as the crystal jellyfish (*Aequorea victoria*) can emit light.

The comb jellyfish (*Ctenophora*), not only produces green and blue lights, but, by moving its tentacles, creates something that looks more like a rainbow! Many believe that this is used to scare away its enemies.

Curiously, the vast majority of animals that can produce their own light do not use it to create light to help them see. Generally, bioluminescence has one of three functions: to search for a mate, to lure prey, or to scare off predators.

Northern Lights

A polar night is when darkness lasts more than 24 hours. This phenomenon only occurs in the Arctic and Antarctic circles on the northernmost and southernmost parts of the Earth. Though some light might be seen due to refraction, the Sun doesn't appear over the horizon for months at a time during polar winter. Imagine spending three months in a place where the Sun does not rise above the horizon at all . . .

The northern lights (sometimes called the aurora borealis) are a spectacular light phenomena. They seem magical, and they occur in areas close to the poles, although there are many exceptions. These are millions of solar particles that come together, forming whimsical shapes in the black sky.

Oxygen is responsible for the colors of the auroras, which are usually green and yellow or orange-red.

We now know that the auroras are physical phenomena, but it is easy to imagine the respect and fear that ancient civilizations must have felt before these celestial projections.

Extraordinary Phenomena

Sometimes the game between the darkness of the night and natural lights produce phenomena that amaze, because they seem magical.

What is an eclipse?

A solar eclipse occurs when the Moon moves into a position that does not allow us to see the Sun from the Earth. As the Moon is smaller than the Sun, this can only happen in situations where the Moon is very close to the Earth.

What is marine bioluminescence?

This occurs when there are a lot of bioluminescent creatures in the water—usually algae or plankton—brought close to the surface by a calm, warm sea. Their presence makes it look as though the ocean is glowing.

What are the pillars of light?

They are visual impressions that are produced when a light source caused by the Sun is reflected in millions of microscopic crystals that float in the air, giving the impression that the beam of light that starts from the Earth rises vertically toward the sky.

Phases of the Moon

The Moon is the Earth's only natural satellite. A satellite is anything that orbits a planet. At 238,855 mi (384,400 km) away, it is the closest celestial body to Earth. The Moon takes 27 days to go around the Earth completely, that's why the phases of the Moon are repeated almost every month.

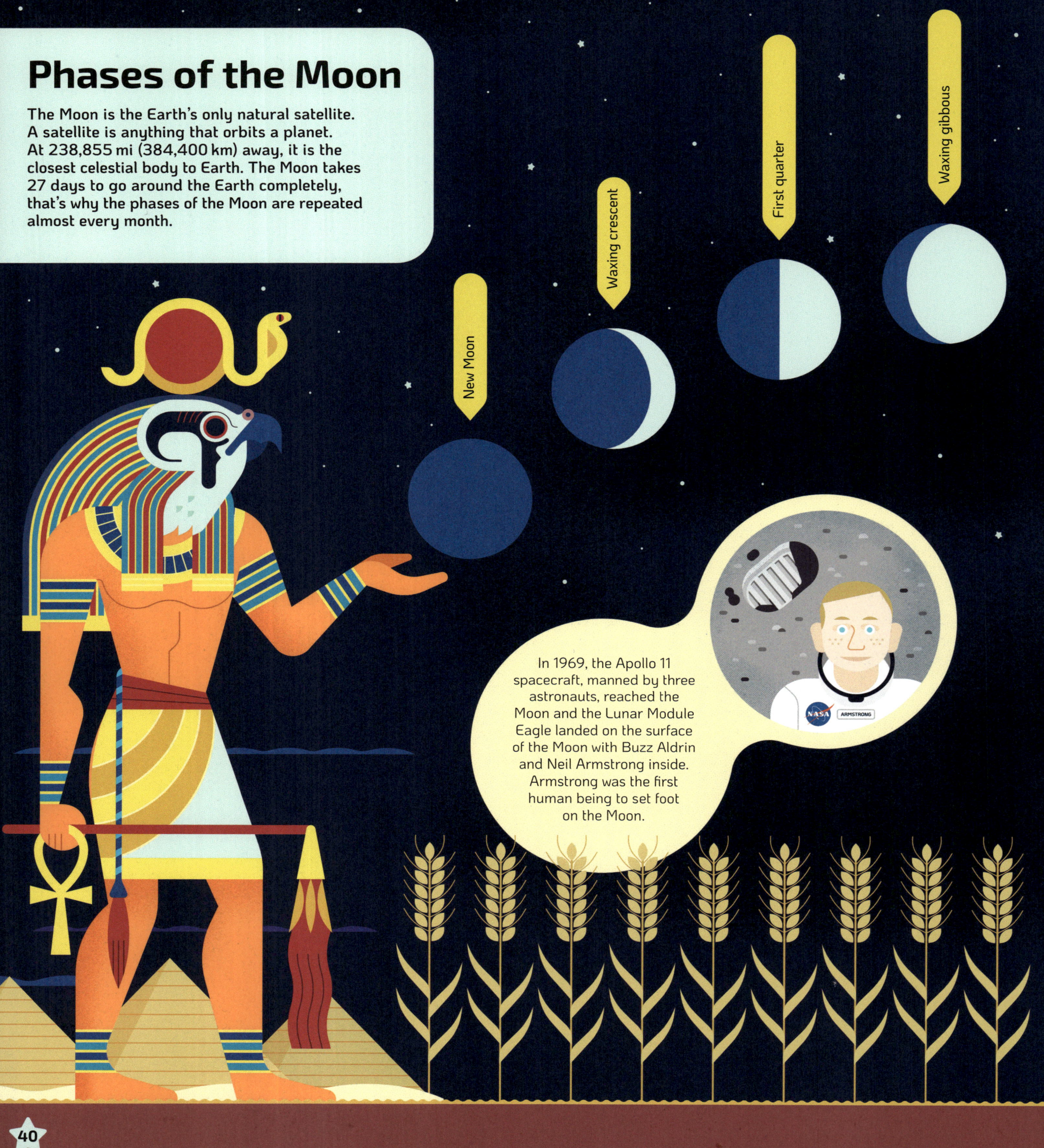

New Moon

Waxing crescent

First quarter

Waxing gibbous

In 1969, the Apollo 11 spacecraft, manned by three astronauts, reached the Moon and the Lunar Module Eagle landed on the surface of the Moon with Buzz Aldrin and Neil Armstrong inside. Armstrong was the first human being to set foot on the Moon.

Full Moon

Waning gibbous

Third quarter

Waning crescent

For thousands of years, humans have been interested in the Moon and the different forms (or phases) it takes in the course of the weeks.

Even before they knew the exact reasons for the lunar phases, many civilizations used the Moon as a calendar for crops or to count time.

If you look closely during a full Moon (if the air is particularly clear), you can sometimes see the craters on the surface of the Moon from the Earth.

Where is the Color at Night?

When light waves hit your retina, your brain is able to identify them. Your eye sends messages to your brain, which interprets them as different colors. Many different living species see colors, but they don't all see them in exactly the same way.

Some people can have disorders, like color blindness, where they see different colors from what most people see.

If there is no light, there are no colors. When there is not even the slightest trace of light, the physical process necessary for us to see the color doesn't happen, so, at that moment, the color does not exist in our mind.

As soon as the first ray of light appears, luckily, the colors return to our lives.

43

Stars, Planets, and Space

Why is there night?

The planet Earth is a satellite of the Sun (it revolves around it), but the Earth also revolves on its axis, so for a few hours a day, it faces the rays of the Sun (daytime) and during some hours, that same point is facing away from the Sun (night).

Why is the Moon only visible at night?

This is not entirely true—we can sometimes see the Moon during the day. Given that it is a satellite of the Earth, but that the Earth does not give off light like the Sun, it is just not always in our view.

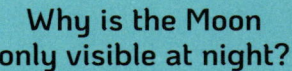

Why is there light on Mars?

We have seen photographs of the surface of Mars and many have been surprised that it appeared to be daytime! Mars is a planet of the solar system, much like Earth, and therefore revolves around the Sun, also rotating on its own axis. Mars has night and day, but the lengths of their days and nights are slightly different to what you experience on Earth.

What is the solar system?

Our solar system is made up of the Sun and the objects that orbit it. This includes our eight planets (Mercury, Venus, Earth, Mars, Jupiter, Saturn, Uranus, and Neptune), dwarf planets (like Pluto), moons, comets, asteroids, and other objects. All of the planets experience night and day (though for different times).

What is the Milky Way?

Our solar system is only a very small part of the universe. We call our home galaxy the Milky Way. There are many, many other galaxies and solar systems in the universe, each with their own suns, planets, satellites etc.

What is a light-year?

The term "light year" does not actually refer to time, but it is used to measure distances. It is the distance that light travels in one year in the vacuum of space, which is approximately 5.8 trillion mi (9.4 trillion km). This means that by the time light reaches the Earth and lets us see into the night sky, the object that we are looking at, for example a star, may have ceased to exist hundreds of years ago.